Contents

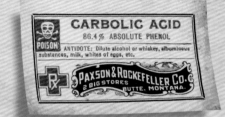

CARBOLIC ACID
86.4% ABSOLUTE PHENOL
POISON
ANTIDOTE: Dilute alcohol or whiskey, albuminous substances, milk, whites of eggs, etc.
PAXSON & ROCKEFELLER CO.
2 BIG STORES
BUTTE, MONTANA.

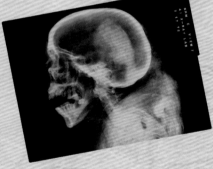

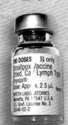

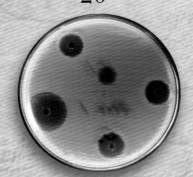

Introduction

The following scientific discoveries have been selected as the Top Ten from thousands of discoveries that have undoubtedly changed our world. Why have these ten made it and not others?

* Firstly, the discovery must have had an impact on the entire world, not just on a part of it.

* Secondly, it must be a scientific discovery rather than an invention (like the telephone).

The discovery of black holes in the 1970s had a huge impact on the scientific world, but didn't affect the world at large.

Alexander Graham Bell's experiments with electrical amplification led him to develop the telephone, an invention rather than a discovery.

THE TOP TEN
SCIENTIFIC
DISCOVERIES
THAT CHANGED THE WORLD

Chris Oxlade

W
FRANKLIN WATTS
LONDON•SYDNEY

This edition published in the UK in 2011 by Franklin Watts

Franklin Watts
338 Euston Road
London NW1 3BH

Franklin Watts Australia
Level 17/207 Kent Street
Sydney, NSW 2000

Dewey classification: 303.4'83

A CIP catalogue record for this book is available from the British Library.

ISBN: 978 1 4451 0644 1

Franklin Watts is a division of Hachette Children's Books, an Hachette UK company.
www.hachette.co.uk

THE TOP TEN SCIENTIFIC DISCOVERIES THAT CHANGED THE WORLD
was produced for Franklin Watts by
David West Children's Books, 7 Princeton Court, 55 Felsham Road, London SW15 1AZ

Copyright © 2009 David West Children's Books

Designer: Gary Jeffrey
Illustrator: David West
Editor: Katharine Pethick

Photographic credits:
4t, Ute Kraus; 7bl, NASA; 7br, Andrew Dunn; 11tr, PHIL; 11b, James Gathany, Nat. Center for
Infectious Diseases; Special Pathogens Branch; 13bl, the_tahoe_guy; 13br, Franco Caruzzo; 15bl,
Library of Congress; 16tl, coxy; 17m, Espino Family; 17br, Library of Congress; 18tl, Lindsay
Holmwood; 19bl, IDuke; 20tl, Duncan Rawlinson; 20bl, Sheep purple; 21mr, PHIL; 21bl, Janice
Carr, Nat. Center for Infectious Diseases; 23mr, NASA, 23br, US Navy; 25ml, Justis- og
politidepartementet; 25bl, Toni Barros

Printed in China

* Thirdly, it must still affect our lives today.

You might disagree with the scientific discoveries that have been chosen here. In that case you could put together a list of those that you think are the most important.

Greek physician Galen's 2nd-century encyclopedia of human anatomy was groundbreaking in its day, but was seriously out of date by the 16th century (left).

SECVNDA SEPTIMI LIBRI FIGVRA'

SECVNDAE FIGVRAE, EIVSDEMQVE CHARA
⁂crum Index,

PRÆSENS figura sectionis serie primam subsequens, tertium duræ membran
sium (quem prima figura C aliquot insignitum gerit) longa sectione secundum capitis longi-
dinem duas deduxi sectiones, utrinque nimirū ad sinum singulas, quæ durum membranam di
gitudinem duas deduxi sectiones, utrinque nimirū ad sinum singulas, quæ durum membranam di
raxat penetravunt, & duræ membrane latera eb ca membrane separarie parte, quæ dextra,
cerebri partem à sinistra dirimit, atque in subsequēti figura tribus D insignietur. Praeter

The Ancient Greek Aristotle (main image) was among the first of the philosophers to promote scientific methods of learning. His discoveries inspired later scientists to carry out their own experiments and investigations.

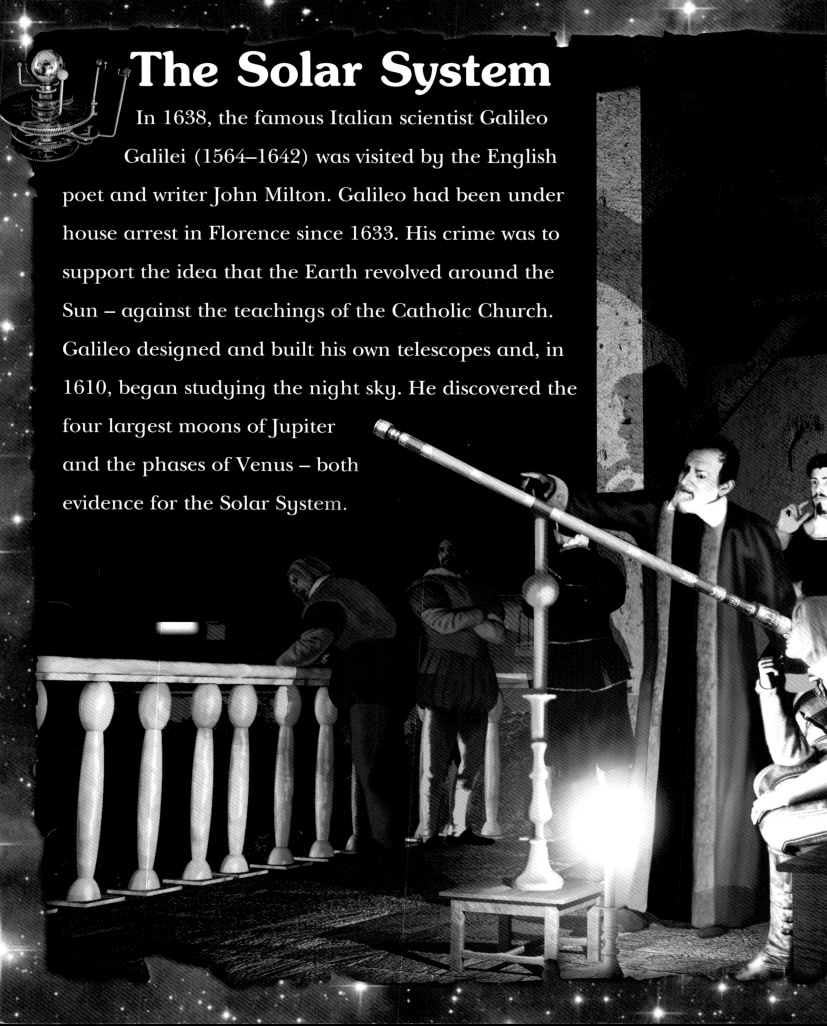

The Solar System

In 1638, the famous Italian scientist Galileo Galilei (1564–1642) was visited by the English poet and writer John Milton. Galileo had been under house arrest in Florence since 1633. His crime was to support the idea that the Earth revolved around the Sun – against the teachings of the Catholic Church. Galileo designed and built his own telescopes and, in 1610, began studying the night sky. He discovered the four largest moons of Jupiter and the phases of Venus – both evidence for the Solar System.

STARS OF ASTRONOMY

In the 15th century, people believed that the Earth was at the centre of the universe and that the Moon,

Sun, planets and stars moved around it. This was mainly because of what the Ancient Greek Ptolemy had written. Polish astronomer Nicolas Copernicus (1473–1543) was the first to question this when he realised that the planets move around the Sun. He also thought that the movement of the stars is caused by the spin of the Earth and that planets move in perfect circles. It was German mathematician Johannes Kepler (1571–1630) who discovered that they actually move in ellipses. **Galileo's discoveries provided the evidence to prove the idea of a Solar System with the Sun at the centre – a huge step forwards in our knowledge about our place in the universe.**

Ptolemy and a 1568 map of the 'Ptolemaic system', with the Earth at the centre

Galileo discovered the rings of Saturn.

Nicolas Copernicus challenged long-held beliefs about the universe.

Isaac Newton (see also pages 8–9) invented the reflecting telescope.

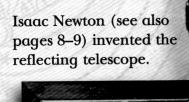

NASA's 1989 probe to Jupiter was named *Galileo* in honour of Galileo's work.

7

Gravity

In the summer of 1684, the astronomer Edmond Halley (1656–1742) visited English scientist Isaac Newton (1642–1727), who was a professor in Cambridge. Halley asked Newton if he would be able to work out how a force of attraction (gravity) made the planets move around the Sun in ellipses. Newton replied that he already had, three years earlier, but had lost the notes he had made. In fact, Newton had developed his law of gravitation nearly 20 years earlier. With Halley's encouragement, he published his theories on gravity and on the motion of objects.

Newton's *Principia*, published in 1687

Newton's laws of motion are used to calculate the forces in machines such as this giant centrifuge.

GRAVITY EVERYWHERE

Newton showed in his law of gravitation that gravity makes every object attract every other object, and that the force depends on the distance between objects. His three laws of motion describe how objects move when they are acted upon by forces. Newton's critical idea was that these laws apply to all objects in the universe – to the planets moving in space as well as to an apple falling from a tree on Earth. Newton also made discoveries about light, invented the reflecting telescope and invented a mathematical tool called calculus. Newton's discovery of gravity remains vital for modern-day scientists in their studies of physics and astronomy.

Science could not have moved forward so far and so fast without Newton's great contribution.

A spacecraft relies on action and reaction – Newton's third law of motion.

The Hubble Space Telescope makes images with a mirror – just as Newton's original telescope did.

In the early 20th century Albert Einstein challenged Newton's theories.

Vaccination

Jenner used a knife to give the first-ever vaccination.

As a doctor in rural England, Edward Jenner (1749–1823) encountered many cases of smallpox, which was a killer, and cowpox, which was unpleasant but not lethal. Milkmaids often caught cowpox from cattle. In the 1790s Jenner made a vital connection. It seemed that people who caught cowpox never got smallpox. Perhaps cowpox could prevent deaths from smallpox. To test his theory, Jenner infected an eight-year-old boy with cowpox. A few weeks later he tried to infect the same boy with smallpox, but the boy didn't catch it. Jenner had discovered vaccination.

Jenner gave a boy cowpox by scratching his hand with a knife carrying material from the skin of an infected milkmaid.

KILLING OFF DISEASES

Edward Jenner hoped that one day his discovery would eradicate smallpox, which at the time killed tens of millions of people each year. In 1979 his wish came true, when the World Health Organisation declared that smallpox had been wiped out by a worldwide vaccination programme.

Vaccines for other killer diseases were gradually discovered and developed. In 1880 Louis Pasteur (see also page 14) accidentally vaccinated some chickens against cholera, and five years later had developed vaccines for anthrax and rabies.

A cartoon from 1812 shows people turning into cows after being vaccinated with cowpox by Jenner.

The terrible effects of smallpox

Today children are routinely vaccinated against several dangerous diseases, including measles, mumps and polio. **Jenner's discovery has literally saved the lives of millions of people in the past 200 years. Its importance for us all cannot be overstated.**

Louis Pasteur (above) developed a vaccine against rabies, which affects animals (right) and humans.

A boy receives a polio vaccination in the 1990s.

Microbiologists are developing new vaccines all the time.

Electromagnetism

In the 19th century, scientists began to discover the link between electricity and magnetism. In 1819, Danish physicist Hans Christian Oersted discovered that a flowing current creates a magnetic field. Armed with this knowledge, Englishman Michael Faraday (1791–1867) discovered that a wire with a current flowing through it would move around a magnet. He went on to make a very simple electric motor in 1821. A decade later, Faraday discovered that moving a magnet in and out of a coil of wire made electricity flow in the wire. This is now known as electromagnetic induction. In the same year, Faraday also invented the electrical transformer.

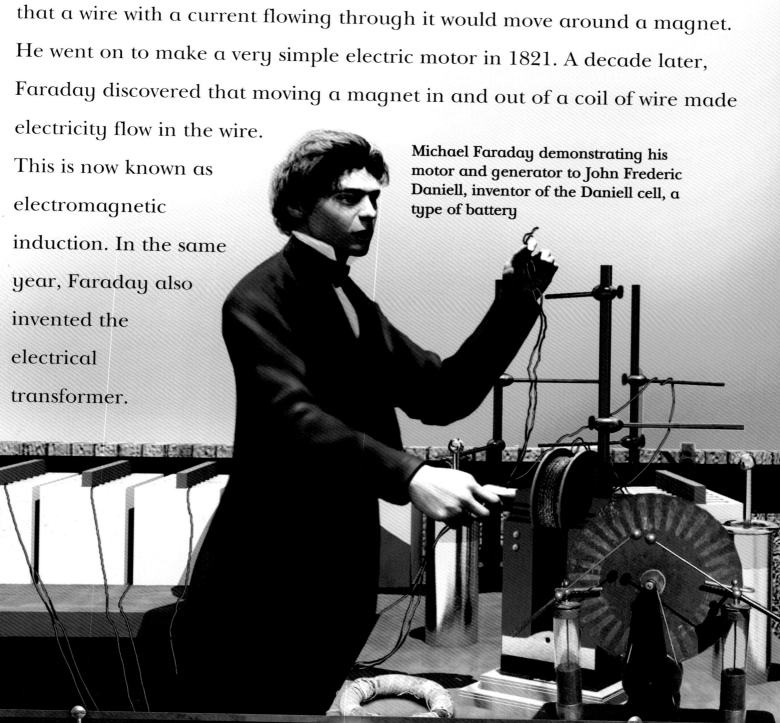

Michael Faraday demonstrating his motor and generator to John Frederic Daniell, inventor of the Daniell cell, a type of battery

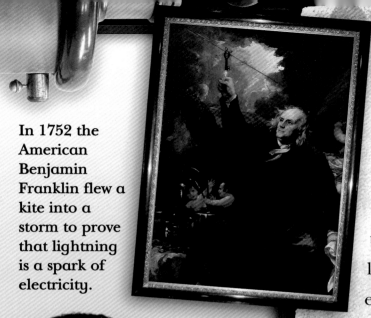

In 1752 the American Benjamin Franklin flew a kite into a storm to prove that lightning is a spark of electricity.

SWITCHED ON

From the 1850s, Faraday's electricity generator was put to use generating electricity for electric arc lamps, which lit some town and city streets. Electricity's big moment was the invention of the filament light bulb. Suddenly everyone wanted electricity to light their bulbs, and the demand led to the construction of the first electricity generating stations in the 1880s. Other wondrous electric appliances, such as irons and ovens, soon began to appear. So did devices that used electric motors to move their parts, such as vacuum cleaners and fans. Electricity was here to stay. **Imagine life without it** today. How many 'essential' gadgets would you have to do without if there were no electricity to power them?

Alessandro Volta's first battery, of 1800

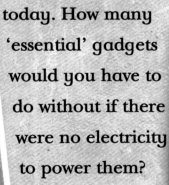

Nikola Tesla invented the induction motor for generating alternating current.

Thomas Edison with an early light bulb

Electricity generators inside the Hoover Dam

Modern society relies very heavily on electricity.

Pasteurisation

In the 1850s, beer and wine often went sour after brewing or fermenting. Producers turned to French chemist Louis Pasteur (1822–95) for help. Using a microscope, Pasteur discovered that a microorganism, brewer's yeast, causes fermentation to produce alcohol. However other microorganisms, such as certain bacteria, produce acid, which makes the drinks sour. Pasteur discovered that heating wine or beer after fermentation to about 63°C for 20 minutes or more kills the unwanted microorganisms, so the drinks keep better. The heating process is now known as pasteurisation. It is used to kill microorganisms in milk and other drinks, cheeses and many other dairy products, as well as in beers and wines.

ORGANISMS IN THE AIR

Pasteur's work on fermentation led him to investigate more closely how microorganisms make food and drink go off. He found that liquids sterilised by boiling do not go off if they are kept in sealed containers, but do go off if left open to the air. This showed him that the microorganisms are in the air and reproduce themselves if they land in food. This dispelled the long-held theory of spontaneous generation, or that microorganisms simply start growing out of nothing.

Pasteur also realised that microorganisms cause many diseases when they get into the body and reproduce. Pasteur also developed vaccines (see page 11). **Pasteur's findings continue to be of vital use to us – we benefit from them each time we drink a glass of milk.**

Microorganisms were discovered in 1674 by Dutchman Anton van Leeuwenhoek using a home-made microscope.

Pasteur used a brass microscope like this one.

Tuberculosis bacteria

PREVENT DISEASE

CARELESS SPITTING, COUGHING, SNEEZING, SPREAD INFLUENZA and TUBERCULOSIS

Microbiology helped conquer bacterial diseases like tuberculosis.

Pasteurisation kills off any dangerous organisms in cows' milk.

Pasteur's discoveries led Joseph Lister to develop antiseptics (see page 16).

15

Antiseptics

Hospital hygiene was nonexistent 150 years ago and patients regularly died from infections after surgery. English surgeon Joseph Lister (1827–1912) changed all that. In the 1860s, he heard about Louis Pasteur's work on infections and microorganisms. Realising that germs must get into the body during surgery, Lister introduced carbolic acid – the first antiseptic. He sprayed it into the air during surgery, soaked dressings with it, and ordered hands and instruments to be cleaned with it. Infections fell dramatically.

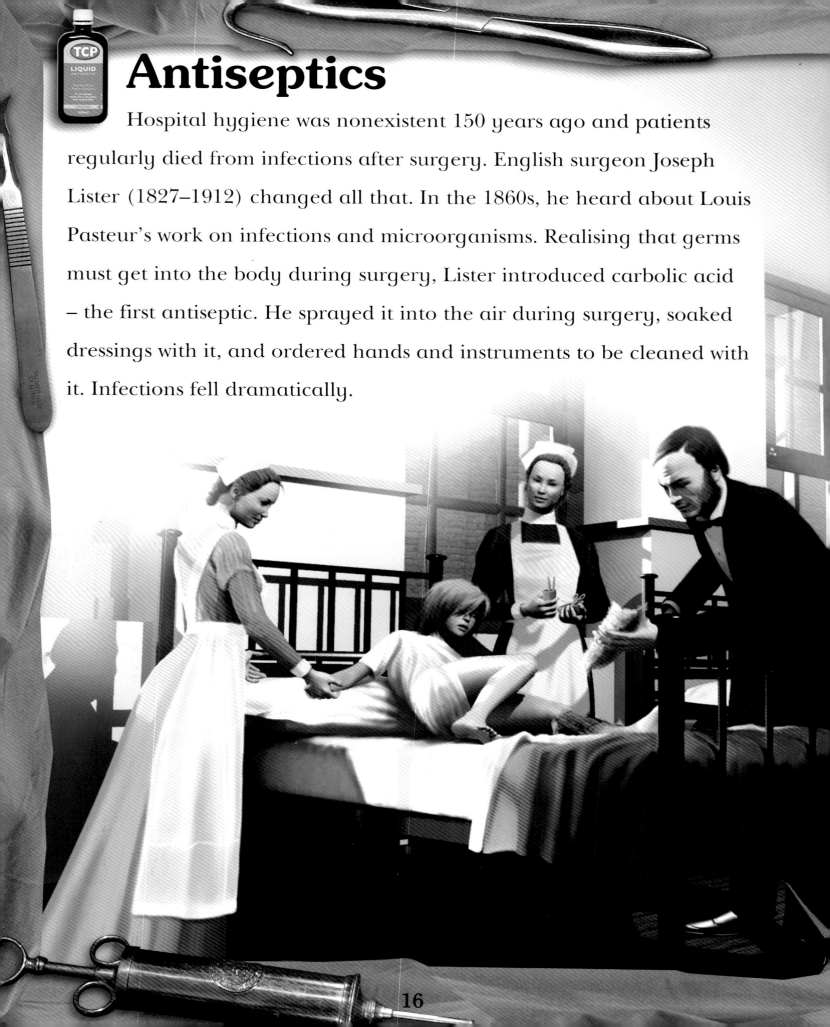

Until Lister's discovery, the importance of surgical hygiene was unknown.

American Oliver Wendell Holmes Junior was one of the first doctors to recommend good hygiene.

WIPING OUT GERMS

Joseph Lister's antiseptic, carbolic acid (now known as phenol), is still used for its antiseptic properties, including cleaning surgeons' hands. Other antiseptics include alcohol, iodine and sodium bicarbonate. Antiseptics are chemicals that kill microorganisms on the surface of the body (antibiotics are used to kill germs inside the body, and disinfectants to kill germs on instruments, work surfaces and so on).

During the Crimean War (1853–55) the nurse Florence Nightingale knew that cleanliness helped to reduce infections.

Lister's carbolic acid sprayer

Today, antiseptics are used in the home in soaps, antiseptic wipes and creams, as well as in mouthwashes. In hospitals they are used to clean wounds and the hands of doctors, nurses and patients, to prevent the spread of diseases. **Modern medicine is made possible by Joseph Lister's discovery. We take safe surgery for granted now – before antiseptics it was always life-threatening.**

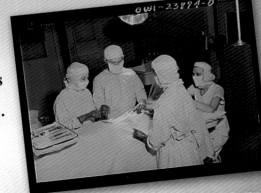

By the middle of the 20th century, operating theatres (right) were completely sterile rooms. Today antiseptics are commonplace (left).

17

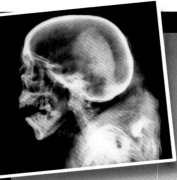

X-rays

In the 1890s, many scientists began studying cathode rays, which had just been discovered. In 1895, Wilhelm Conrad Röntgen (1845–1923) was experimenting with a cathode ray tube (a sealed glass tube inside which cathode rays were made) covered with black paper. In his darkened laboratory, he noticed that a chemical-coated screen, a metre from the tube, was glowing. Röntgen knew the cathode rays could not reach that far, and he realised he had discovered a new type of ray, created when the cathode rays hit the glass tube. He called them X-rays. Critically, he discovered that X-rays can pass right through many materials, including flesh. Armed with this knowledge, Röntgen took an X-ray photograph of the bones in his wife's hand – the first-ever medical X-ray.

SEEING THE INVISIBLE

X-rays took the medical world by storm. Here a patient's bones are revealed by X-rays energising a fluorescent screen.

Röntgen's discovery was quickly put to use by the medical profession. For the first time they could see inside their patients' bodies without opening them up. However, several scientists died from cancers caused by overexposure to X-rays, before the dangers were properly understood. In the 1970s, the computerised axial tomography (CAT or CT) scanner was developed. This uses X-rays to build a 3-D image of a patient's internal organs. X-rays are also used to treat tumours caused by cancer. Outside medicine, engineers use X-rays to spot faults in metals and scientists use them to detect atoms.

Röntgen's X-rays were produced by a cathode ray tube developed by Englishman Sir William Crookes.

Most modern X-ray tubes are Coolidge tubes, developed in 1913.

Marie Curie built X-ray machines for use in the First World War.

From finding a hairline crack in a bone to treating serious illnesses, Röntgen's X-rays help keep us safe in many different ways.

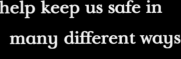

Airport security scanners look inside luggage using X-rays.

Modern body scanners show the human body in extraordinary detail.

19

Penicillin

British Army doctor Alexander Fleming (1881–1955) witnessed the deaths of many First World War soldiers from infections and decided to search for a way of fighting these infections. Fleming's breakthrough discovery came in 1928. After returning from holiday, Fleming examined dishes of bacteria. A lid was missing from one of them. As well as bacteria, a mould called *Penicillium notatum* was growing in it. The bacteria around the mould were dead. A chemical from the mould was acting as an antibiotic, meaning it was killing bacteria.

Today there are several antibiotics based on penicillin.

BACTERIA KILLERS

The fact that the *Penicillium* mould kills bacteria was first noticed in 1845 by John Tyndall.

Alexander Fleming named his new antibiotic penicillin. Unfortunately he could not find a way to make it in large enough quantities to be used widely as an antibiotic. A manufacturing method was finally developed in 1939 by two other scientists, Howard Walter Florey and Ernst Boris Chain and their team at Oxford University. Fleming, Florey and Chain, shared the Nobel Prize for Medicine in 1945.

Before antibiotics were found, maggots were used to clean wounds.

Penicillin played an important role in fighting disease during the Second World War.

Today there are more than 100 different antibiotics available, both natural and artificial. But drug designers are kept on their toes because bacteria gradually become resistant to antibiotics. **Fleming's penicillin is still in regular use. It has saved countless lives, as well as curing childhood infections in almost everyone.**

Antibiotics are not a cure-all. Some bacteria, such as MRSA, are resistant to them.

Nuclear Power

In the 1930s, physicists were investigating the structure of atoms. They discovered that some atoms absorb neutrons fired at them. In 1938 two German scientists, Otto Hahn (1879–1968) and Fritz Strassmann (1902–80), were bombarding uranium with neutrons and were amazed to find that some uranium atoms had split completely in two, forming atoms of barium and krypton. They also found that a large amount of energy was released. By chance they had discovered nuclear fission – splitting the atom.

Hahn and Strassmann did not realise they had set off a nuclear chain reaction.

Lise Meitner worked with Hahn and Strassmann, but left Germany after the Nazis rose to power in 1938. Her vital role in the discovery of nuclear fission was never officially recognised.

THE RACE FOR A BOMB

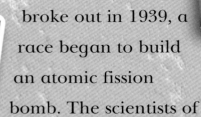

'Fat Man', the bomb dropped on Nagasaki in 1945

When the Second World War broke out in 1939, a race began to build an atomic fission bomb. The scientists of the USA's Manhattan Project exploded the first atomic bomb in July 1945. In August that year atomic bombs were dropped on the Japanese cities of Hiroshima and Nagasaki. In the 1950s, at the start of the Cold War, the USA and the Soviet Union developed the more powerful fusion or hydrogen bomb. At the same time nuclear technology was being put to peacetime use with the development of nuclear reactors to produce electricity. **Today,** about 15 per cent of the world's electricity is generated by nuclear power – a great boon in a world that's running out of power.

The world's first nuclear reactor, Chicago Pile 1, built in 1942

An experimental nuclear reactor lit four light bulbs in 1952.

A missile carrying a nuclear warhead. During the Cold War thousands of these weapons were manufactured.

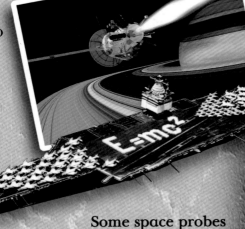

Some space probes and ships are nuclear powered.

Inside a nuclear reactor, showing the rods of uranium fuel

The Secret of Life

In 1953, Englishman Francis Crick (1916–2004) and American James Dewey Watson (b. 1928) were trying to decipher the structure of a fantastically complex chemical called DNA. Almost every cell of every living thing contains DNA. It contains instructions, known as genes, that control what living things look like and how they work. At last the breakthrough came when a fellow scientist, Rosalind Franklin, shared her research work with them. Just a few weeks later, they announced that they had found 'the secret of life'.

Crick and Watson discovered that DNA is a double helix – like a twisted rope ladder.

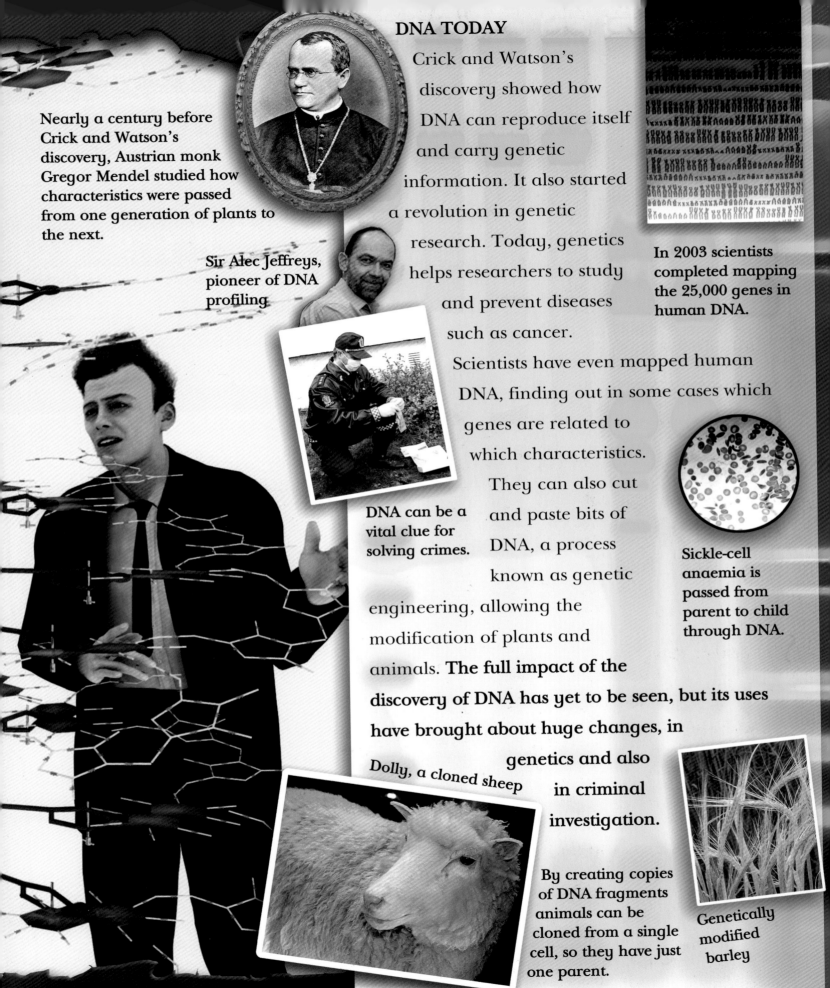

DNA TODAY

Nearly a century before Crick and Watson's discovery, Austrian monk Gregor Mendel studied how characteristics were passed from one generation of plants to the next.

Sir Alec Jeffreys, pioneer of DNA profiling

Crick and Watson's discovery showed how DNA can reproduce itself and carry genetic information. It also started a revolution in genetic research. Today, genetics helps researchers to study and prevent diseases such as cancer.

Scientists have even mapped human DNA, finding out in some cases which genes are related to which characteristics. They can also cut and paste bits of DNA, a process known as genetic engineering, allowing the modification of plants and animals. **The full impact of the discovery of DNA has yet to be seen, but its uses have brought about huge changes, in genetics and also in criminal investigation.**

DNA can be a vital clue for solving crimes.

In 2003 scientists completed mapping the 25,000 genes in human DNA.

Sickle-cell anaemia is passed from parent to child through DNA.

Dolly, a cloned sheep

By creating copies of DNA fragments animals can be cloned from a single cell, so they have just one parent.

Genetically modified barley

The Best of the Rest

FIRE

Early humans must have seen natural forest and grass fires, probably ignited by lightning. At first they may have lit their own fires from natural fires. They used fire to cook food, to make light (especially those who lived in caves), to ward off wild animals and to keep warm as they migrated to live in colder climates. The most useful discovery was how to start a fire at will. At some point, probably hundreds of thousands of years ago, people found that rubbing sticks together created enough heat to start a fire and that striking certain rocks together made sparks that could ignite material.

Early tools for lighting fire included pieces of flint and flammable fungus.

METALS

The first materials people had for manufacturing were natural ones around them – wood, animal skins and bones, stone and clay. Around 10,000 years ago people began making small items from naturally occurring deposits of metals, such as copper and gold. But the groundbreaking discovery was how to extract metals from their ores by smelting. Copper and tin were discovered first, about 6000 BC, and combined to make bronze, which was used to make tools, weapons and jewellery. Then sometime after 1500 BC people discovered how to smelt iron. Iron proved to be stronger than bronze so was ideal for making tools and weapons. The age of metal really had arrived.

The discovery of iron smelting revolutionised warfare.

ARCHIMEDES PRINCIPLE

Archimedes (c. 287–212 BC) was a Greek scientist, mathematician and inventor. He discovered a scientific fact now known as the Archimedes principle. This states that a liquid pushes upwards on an object with a force equal to the weight of the liquid that the pushed object displaces. The principle explains why objects float.

Amongst Archimedes' inventions is the Archimedean screw, still used to raise water.

THE HUMAN BODY

In ancient times, scientists and doctors knew ways of making people better and healing wounds, but their theories about how the body works were largely wrong. Proper scientific

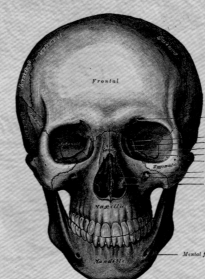

Henry Gray wrote the famous medical reference book *Gray's Anatomy*, still in use today.

Dr Henry Gray

Drawings of the human body made by Leonardo da Vinci.

investigation of the human body began in the 16th century, when Andreas Vesalius made detailed drawings of the human body from dissections he performed. In the early 17th century, William Harvey discovered that the heart pumps blood around the body and, in the 19th century, Theodor Schwann discovered that the human body is made up of countless cells. A great many more discoveries by numerous scientists since have built up the detailed knowledge we have today.

Ether was first used by dentists in the 1840s.

ANAESTHESIA

Until the discovery of anaesthesia patients were awake during surgery. It was extremely painful and sufferers had to be held down to keep them still. Then, in the middle of the 19th century, dentists and physicians discovered that the gases nitrous oxide and ether both acted as anaesthetics when they where inhaled. The dentists doing experiments included Dr Horace Wells, who proved the effectiveness of nitrous oxide by using it on himself so that a fellow dentist could extract one of his teeth.

EVOLUTION

In the early 19th century scientists knew from fossils that animals and plants slowly change over time. Over millions of years some species die out and new species appear. But nobody knew why these changes happen. The answer was discovered by English naturalist Charles Darwin (1809–82). As a naturalist on the survey ship HMS *Beagle*, Darwin observed thousands of animals and plants. The way in which many were adapted to their surroundings convinced him that there are small changes from one generation to the next, but only the animals with useful changes survive – his theory of evolution by natural selection. Another naturalist, Alfred Russel Wallace, had the same theory and so the two revealed their ideas together.

Darwin's notes on natural selection

Darwin's ideas were hugely controversial when they were published in 1859 because they suggested that humans are related to apes.

In the 1860s Dmitry Mendeleyev realised that many elements were still to be discovered.

By the middle of the 19th century, 60 were known. Russian chemist Dmitry Mendeleyev organised the elements into a table according to their properties and found that there were gaps. He predicted that elements would be discovered to fill the gaps and he was proved right.

THE ELEMENTS

Today we know that all materials are made up of chemical elements, and that elements combine to make thousands of different materials. Some elements, including copper, gold and sulphur, have been known for thousands of years because they can be found in a pure form in nature. But ancient people also considered water and air to be elements. In the 18th century, scientists began to discover that air and water are made up of other elements, including oxygen and hydrogen. Gradually more and more elements were discovered.

RELATIVITY

In the early 20th century, Albert Einstein (1879–1955) published some amazing new theories, including his famous theories of relativity. For example, they stated that Newton's laws of motion (see page 9) are not true for objects that travel near the speed of light, and that energy and mass can be converted to each other. In 1921, Einstein received the Nobel Prize for his various theories. His theories have helped us to understand the origin and fate of the Universe.

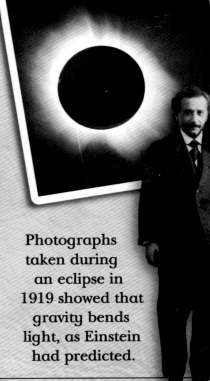

Photographs taken during an eclipse in 1919 showed that gravity bends light, as Einstein had predicted.

Timeline of Scientific Discoveries

		The Discovery	The Scientists
ANCIENT	98,000 BC	FIRE	Unknown
	6000 BC	COPPER SMELTING	People of modern-day Middle East
	4000 BC	BRONZE	People of modern-day Middle East
	1500 BC	IRON SMELTING	Possibly India
	250 BC	THE ARCHIMEDES PRINCIPLE	Archimedes (c. 287–212 BC) The Greek mathematician, physicist, engineer, and inventor
MEDIEVAL/MODERN ERAS	1609	PLANETS TRAVEL IN ELLIPSES	Johannes Kepler (1571–1630), German mathematician
	1610	**THE MOONS OF JUPITER**	**Galileo Galilei (1564–1642), Italian scientist and astronomer**
	1628	THE CIRCULATORY SYSTEM	William Harvey (1578–1657), English doctor
	1674	MICROORGANISMS	Anton van Leeuwenhoek (1632–1723), Dutch textile dealer
	1684	**THE LAW OF GRAVITATION**	**Isaac Newton (1642–1727), English scientist and mathematician**
	1790s	**VACCINATION**	**Edward Jenner (1749–1823), English doctor**
	1800	THE PRINCIPLE OF THE BATTERY	Alessandro Volta (1745–1827), Italian scientist
	1821	**THE MOTOR EFFECT**	**Michael Faraday (1791–1867), English chemist and physicist**
	1850s	**PASTEURISATION**	**Louis Pasteur (1822–95), French chemist**
	1859	NATURAL SELECTION	Charles Darwin (1809–82), Alfred Russel Wallace (1823–1913), English naturalists
	1860s	**ANTISEPTICS**	**Joseph Lister (1827–1912), English surgeon**
	1895	**X-RAYS**	**Wilhelm Conrad Röntgen (1845–1923), German physicist**
20TH CENTURY	1909	RELATIVITY	Albert Einstein (1879–1955), German-born physicist
	1928	**PENICILLIN**	**Alexander Fleming (1881–1955), Scottish doctor**
	1939	**ATOMIC FISSION (SPLITTING THE ATOM)**	**Otto Hahn (1879–1968), Fritz Strassman (1902–80), German physicists, Lise Meitner (1878–1968), Austrian-Swedish physicist**
	1953	**THE STRUCTURE OF DNA**	**Francis Crick (1916–2004), English biologist, James Dewey Watson (b. 1928), American biologist**
	1970s	BLACK HOLES	Various astronomers

The Result

Provided warmth, light, protection and heat for cooking

Allowed use of copper for making tools and jewellery

Allowed manufacture of tough weapons and tools

Began the widespread use of iron

Explained the upwards push on objects in a liquid

Explained the movement of the planets across the night sky

Evidence for the structure of the Solar System

Showed the function of the heart, arteries and veins

Showed that a whole world of microorganisms existed

Showed why the planets move in elliptical orbits and why things fall to Earth

Protected people from the killer disease smallpox

The first battery – a source of electricity

The principle of the electric motor

Improved brewing and killed germs in drinks

Revolutionised thinking on the evolution of animals

Prevented infections during hospital surgery

Allowed doctors to look inside their patients without surgery

---

Revolutionised the study of physics and astronomy

The first successful antibiotic for treating infections

Made possible atomic weapons and atomic power

Began the genetic revolution and genetic engineering

Confirmed the existence of objects in space so dense that light cannot escape

Glossary

Alternating current An electric current that flows alternately one way, then the other way

Antiseptic A substance used to kill microorganisms in wounds or on the skin

Atom The particles that all substances are made from. They cannot usually be broken up

Cathode ray A stream of particles called electrons

Displace To push out of the way

Element A substance that cannot be broken down into simpler substances

Ellipse A shape like a squashed circle

Fission The process of an atom splitting into separate parts, forming smaller atoms

Fusion The process of two atoms joining together, forming a single larger atom

Gravity The force that attracts every object to every other object, including you to the Earth

Microorganism A microscopically small organism invisible to the naked eye

Neutron One of the tiny particles that make up atoms (the others are protons and electrons)

Reflecting telescope A telescope that gathers light using a curved mirror

Smelting Extracting metals from minerals (ores) by heating them to a high temperature

Vaccine A substance that causes a mild disease in a person, but then protects him or her from a more virulent disease

Index